AGE 7-9

Spelling Practice

Exercises devised by Nicola Morgan
an experienced teacher and educational consultant
Illustrated by Pip Adams

About this book

Spelling Practice 7-9 forms part of **Learning Rewards**, a home-learning programme designed to help your child succeed at school with the National Curriculum (and with the 5-14 programme in Scotland). It has been extensively researched with parents and teachers.

Children should start with the Skills books and progress to the Practice books

| English Skills | Spelling Skills | Writing Skills |

Skills Books
Introduce the basic skills through worked examples and parent notes

| English Practice | Spelling Practice | Writing Practice |

Practice Books
Consolidate and reinforce the basic skills through repeated exercises

The whole set covers important aspects of the National Curriculum during Years 3 and 4

How to use this book

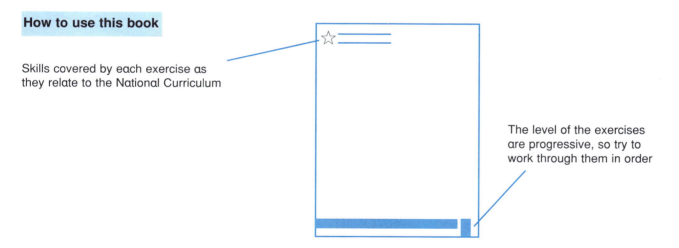

Skills covered by each exercise as they relate to the National Curriculum

The level of the exercises are progressive, so try to work through them in order

How you can help

- Work through each page with your child and talk about what is required
- Always work at your child's pace and give lots of praise
- Record your child's performance using the progress chart and gold stickers

Published in Great Britain in 2002, by Egmont Books Ltd.
239 Kensington High Street, London, W8 6SA.
Printed in Italy
3 5 7 9 10 8 6 4

ISBN 0 7498 5575 4

How we learn to spell

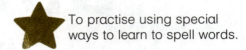
To practise using special ways to learn to spell words.

Remember: when several words have the same pattern, learn them together.

Sort these words into two groups and write them in the cloud or the whale.

loud ✓   white   wheel   proud ✓   whether
snout ✓   whiskers   whip   doubtful ✓   couch ✓

whale
white
whiskers
wheel
whip
whether

cloud
Loud
proud
couch
snout
doubtful

Remember: when a word is tricky or doesn't fit a pattern, learn it like this:

LOOK at it   **SAY** the letters   **COVER** it   **WRITE** it   **CHECK** it

Use this method to learn to spell these words:

through
through ~~thought~~
special
Special
ghost
ghost

straight
Straight
different
different
exciting
exciting

doubt
doubt
favourite
favourite
weird
weird

Put a star by each one when you can spell it easily.

 To practise using a dictionary and alphabetical order.

Using a dictionary

Put the list in alphabetical order. Remember: if the first letters are the same, try the second letters. If they're the same, try the third. And so on.

carrot	1. _Cabbage_
cabbage	2. _carrot_
cauliflower	3. _caterpillar_
crab	4. _Cauliflower_
crayfish	5. _clam_
caterpillar	6. _crab_
clam	7. _crayfish_

Some of these are spelt wrongly. Check them with the dictionary on page 31. Write the word correctly. Then write the NEXT word from the dictionary list.

	correction	next word
tommorrow	tomorrow ✓	towards ✓
dissappear	disappear ✓	disappoint ✓
sensible	d	silliness ✓
sylable	syllable ✓	televison
important	—	interesting ✓
dificult	difficult ✓	disappear

good work Thomasina.

Vowels and consonants

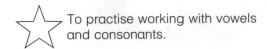

To practise working with vowels and consonants.

Remember: the vowels are **a, e, i, o, u**.
We call the other letters 'consonants'. **y** is special: it can be both.

Fill in the missing vowels to read this sentence:

When Dad got to the shop,
he forgot why he had come,
so he went home to ask Mum.
She just laughed. "You went to buy a
notepad to help you remember things," she said.

When a vowel sounds like its own NAME,
we say it is LONG. **a** as in ape
When it sounds like the letter SOUND,
we say it is SHORT. **a** as in apple

Circle the words with LONG vowel sounds in blue.
Circle the words with SHORT vowel sounds in red.

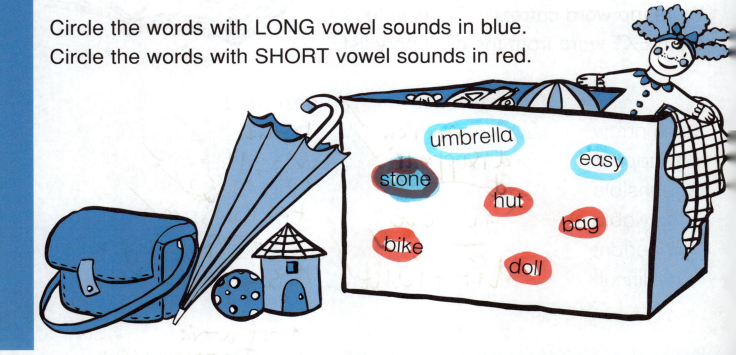

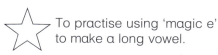

To practise using 'magic e' to make a long vowel.

Practising 'magic e'

These words have a short vowel. Put **e** on the end and read the words aloud.

Now the vowel makes a long sound.

rate   site   note

hate   pine   spine

spite   tube   tripe

Answer these clues with 'magic **e**' words.
The shaded letters will spell a word –
that's you!

				c	o	n	e
			s	a	l	e	
		t	u	n	e		
			d	i	v	e	r
	s	k	a	t	e		
			p	r	i	z	e

1. You might eat ice-cream in this.
2. When a shop cuts its prices.
3. The notes of a song make this.
4. Someone who swims deep under water.
5. You do this on ice.
6. Someone who wins a race might get one.

clever

5

Spelling with **tch** and **ch**

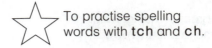

To practise spelling words with **tch** and **ch**.

Remember: after a short vowel, write **tch**. After a long vowel write **ch**.
Remember that these words don't follow the rule:

rich   **much**   **such**   **which**

Can you write a sentence using all these words:
witch, rich, itch, which.

_____

Fill in the gaps in this story with words that end in **tch** or **ch**.
The correct number of spaces for each letter of the word are there
to help you.

Last week s _ _ _ a wonderful thing happened. I went to w_ _ _ _ _
a football m _ _ _ _ _ with my mum and dad. The ball came right to
me and I had to c _ _ _ _ _ it and throw it back onto the p _ _ _ _ _.
At half-time the team c _ _ _ _ _ said I could sit on the b _ _ _ _ _
with him. Afterwards, e _ _ _ _ member of the team shook my hand
and said thank you very m _ _ _ _ , w _ _ _ _ _ was something I will
remember all my life

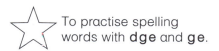

To practise spelling words with **dge** and **ge**.

Spelling with **dge** and **ge**

Remember: after a short vowel, write **dge**.

After a long vowel, write **ge**.

The word 'vegetable' is different.

Practise writing 'vegetable' using the LOOK, SAY method.

_____

_____

Here is a wordsearch with lots of **dge** and **ge** words. Write all the ones you can find in the correct spaces. Some letters are already there to help you. Remember that words may go up, down, forwards, backwards, across or diagonally.

fri _ _ _   lo _ _ _   gor _ _   po _ _ _ _ _ _

he _ _ _ _ _ _   sto _ _ _   ed _ _   we _ _ _

ca _ _   pa _ _   hu _ _   ra _ _

ag _   sta _ _   do _ _ _   wa _ _

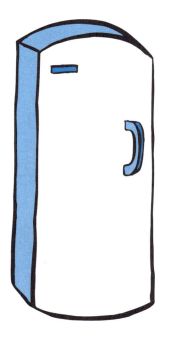

f	r	i	d	g	e	w	s	h
s	r	t	e	m	a	s	d	u
e	h	e	d	g	e	h	o	g
g	s	g	e	e	e	c	d	e
a	l	a	e	g	a	a	g	s
p	o	r	r	i	d	g	e	n
s	d	o	r	d	t	e	a	s
e	g	d	o	t	s	a	w	s
d	e	g	a	t	s	e	s	w

7

Learning about syllables

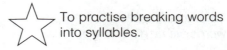

To practise breaking words into syllables.

Remember: if you don't know how to spell a longer word, break it into syllables.

Count the syllables in these words:

computer ___   syllable ___   telephone ___   sensible ___

Can you fill the spaces? Page 31 will help you.

1. The new school term starts t _ _ _ r r _ _.
2. I did not u _ _ _ _ s _ _ _ d what he meant.
3. It is very im _ _ _ _ _ _ _ to wear a cycle helmet.
4. She waved her wand and d i _ _ p p _ _ _ _ _.
5. We went on h _ _ _ _ _ _ to Spain last summer.
6. I write things down to help me r _ _ _ _ _ _ _ .
7 The ambulance took him to h _ _ _ _ _ _ _.

8

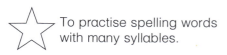 To practise spelling words with many syllables.

Spell these words by splitting them into syllables.

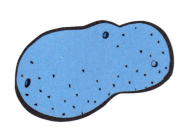

p _ /_ _/_ _

c _ _/_ _/_ _/_ _

a _/_ _/_ _ _

Make some long words using one syllable from each column.
Check them on page 31 because some are tricky.

be	ic	at
cel	fort	al
ex	gin	y
ac	ci	rate
dis	ter	point
typ	eb	ing
com	ap	ting
mys	rob	ning

_____

_____

_____

_____

_____

_____

_____

_____

Which word do you most want to be able to spell?
Use the method:
LOOK,   SAY,   COVER,   WRITE,_____ CHECK

Vowel endings

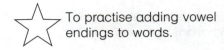
To practise adding vowel endings to words.

Some suffixes (endings) start with a vowel.
We call them 'vowel endings'. When you add a vowel ending to a word that ends in **e**, drop the **e** first.
In spelling rules, **y** counts as a vowel.

Fill the white boxes by adding the endings and dropping the **e** if necessary.

You can check your answers on page 31.

	ing	er	ed	y
phone				
jump				
smile				
bone				
creep				
tickle				
scare				
love				

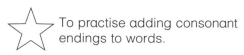 To practise adding consonant endings to words.

Other suffixes start with a consonant and are called 'consonant endings'.

Don't drop the **e** before a consonant ending.

But if a word ends in **y**, change the **y** to **i**.

happy + ly = happily

Work out how to make these words:

funny + ly = _____   silly + ness = _____

pity + ful = _____   lovely + ness = _____

Add these consonant endings. Remember about **y**.
Check your answers on page 3l.

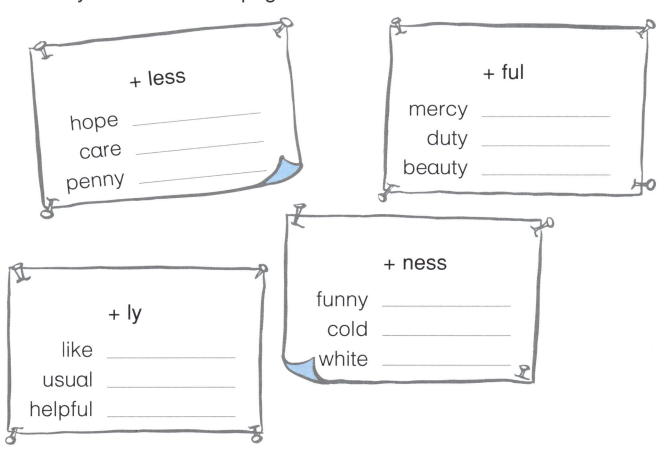

+ less

hope _____
care _____
penny _____

+ ful

mercy _____
duty _____
beauty _____

+ ly

like _____
usual _____
helpful _____

+ ness

funny _____
cold _____
white _____

More prefixes and suffixes

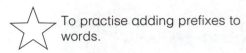 To practise adding prefixes to words.

Remember: **all**, **full** and **till** drop one **l** when we add them to another word.

For example: **always** **useful** **until**

Write a sentence using all these words:

also, helpful, although, useful.

_____

Answer the clues and discover another word in the blue column.

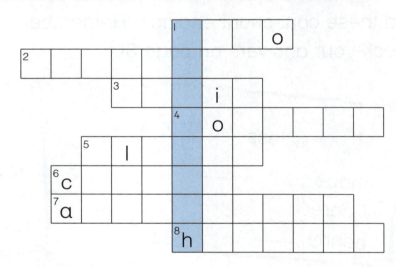

1. As well
2. Opposite of useless
3. "Wait _____ I come back."
4. Feeling that good news will come
5. Not quite
6. As much as you can put in one cup
7. Completely
8. As much as you can hold in one hand

The word in the blue column is _____ .

☆ To practise identifying a word's root.

The root word

The **root** is the word we start with before adding prefixes and suffixes.
The root of 'disentangling' is 'tangle' – this was the start of the word before we added **dis**, **en** and **ing** to it.
The root tells us that 'disentangling' has something to do with 'tangle'.

Take away the prefixes and suffixes to find the roots of these words.

disproving	overacting	disgraceful
— — — — —	— — —	— — — —
unprompted	unfairly	downloading
— — — — — —	— — — —	— — — —
misguided	uplifting	uneasily
— — — — —	— — — —	— — — —

Can you think of a word that you could add to these prefixes?

un _____   mis _____   im _____

under _____   tele _____   dis _____

Can you write a sentence using the word **disgraceful**?

_____
_____
_____
_____

Useful words to learn

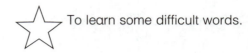 To learn some difficult words.

Remember: some words are not spelt as they sound. We have to learn them using LOOK, SAY, COVER, WRITE, CHECK.

The words in the balloons are very useful.

Practise each word. When you can spell each one, colour its balloon.

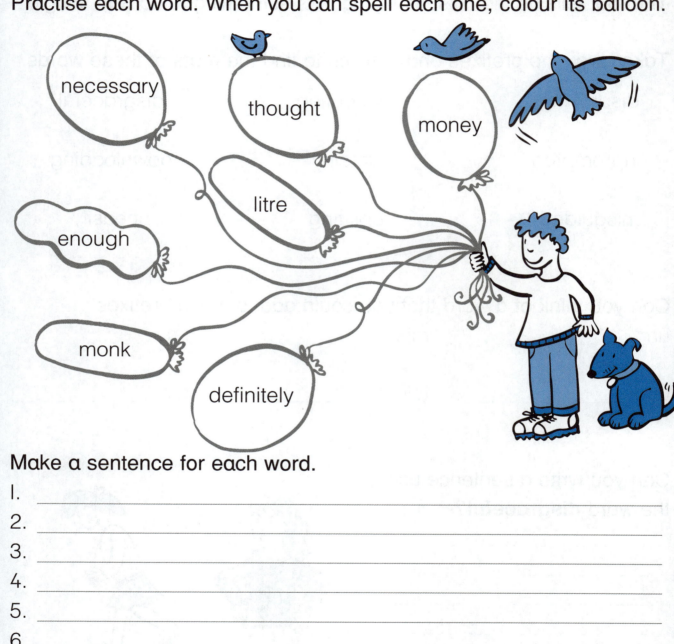

Make a sentence for each word.

1. _____
2. _____
3. _____
4. _____
5. _____
6. _____
7. _____

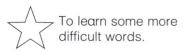
To learn some more
difficult words.

Write one of these words in the vapour trail.

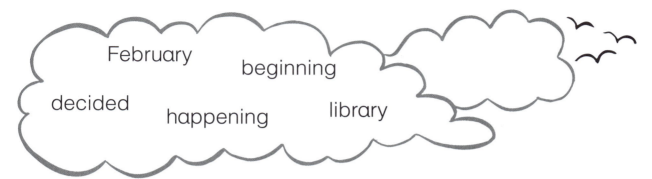

February

beginning

decided

happening

library

Practise spelling it using LOOK, SAY, COVER, WRITE, CHECK.
Then do the same with the others.

Write a sentence for two of the words.

1. _____

2. _____

Different spelling, same sound

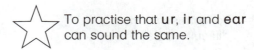

To practise that **ur**, **ir** and **ear** can sound the same.

Listen for words with the sound **ur**.
(They may be spelt with **ur**, **ir** or **ear**).
Write each one under the correct sound.

The clown dressed as a bird for his circus turn. On the third day, he burnt his beak, which hurt. He learnt that this was a silly way to earn money and now he is searching for a new job. He heard about a job thirty miles away and it turned out to be the best job he could imagine.

ur	ir	ear
_____	_____	_____
_____	_____	_____
_____	_____	_____
_____	_____	_____

Spelling

☆ To practise words ending in **ous**.

Remember: words ending in the sound 'us' are usually spelt with **ous**.

Match the words to their correct meanings.

enormous	very careful
courageous	worth a lot of money
cautious	rich, comfortable and expensive
jealous	worried
precious	well-known by lots of people
luxurious	strange; can also mean 'nosey'
dangerous	brave
curious	huge
anxious	wanting what someone else has got
famous	not safe, risky

Make interesting sentences using:

cautious _____

luxurious _____

anxious _____

Plurals

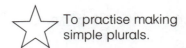

To practise making simple plurals.

Remember these rules for plural endings:

1. If the plural sounds like **is**, add **es**
2. Words that end in **o**, usually add **es**.
3. If a word ends in **consonant + y**, change **y** to **i** and add **es**.
4. If it ends in **vowel + y**, add **s**.

Write the plurals for these words. Check your answers using page 31.

donkey   _ _ _ _ _ _ _   valley   _ _ _ _ _ _ _

bus   _ _ _ _ _   hero   _ _ _ _ _ _

day   _ _ _ _   rush   _ _ _ _ _ _ _

army   _ _ _ _ _ _

house   _ _ _ _ _ _

echo   _ _ _ _ _ _

Turn the nouns into plurals:

The <u>monkey</u> sat on a <u>bush</u> eating a <u>tomato</u>.

_____

The <u>dictionary</u> did not have the <u>word</u> the <u>boy</u> wanted.

_____

To practise more complicated plurals.

Remember: most words that end in **f** or **fe** change to **ves**.
And some other words become very different in the plural.

Fill the spaces, and check your answers on page 31.

One wife, two _ _ _ _ _ _

A child, five _ _ _ _ _ _ _ _ _

A wolf, a pack of _ _ _ _ _ _ _

One life, nine _ _ _ _ _ _

One man, lots of _ _ _ _

One half, two _ _ _ _ _ _ _

One woman, some _ _ _ _ _ _ _

One loaf, five _ _ _ _ _ _ _

These words DON'T follow the rule for – **f**. They just add **s**. So do all words ending – **ff**.

reef – **reefs**   chief – **chiefs**   belief – **beliefs**   surf – **surfs**

Close the book. Can you remember those words?

Write two sentences using as many of these plurals as you can.

1. _____

2. _____

Listening to **igh** and **ough**

Use this spelling wheel
to see how many **igh** words
you can make.

_____

_____

_____

_____

_____

l

n

s

t

br

igh

ting

f

fr

ter

t

th

_____

_____

_____

_____

The **ough** pattern in these
words looks the same but
makes different sounds.

enough   dough

although   bought   trough

thought   ought

Put the right **ough** word in each space.

I th _____ I had e _____ flour to make d_____ ,
a _____ I really o _____ to have b_____ more.

One word is left. Can you write a sentence for it?

_____

Spelling

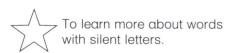

To learn more about words with silent letters.

Circle the silent letters in these words.

thistle   wheel   bomb   autumn   listen   ghost

column   lamb   hymn   thumb   bristle   which

Sort the words into the correct hat.

b

t

h

n

Here are three more: doubt   thought   knight

Can you put each one in a sentence?

1. _____

2. _____

3. _____

Same sound, different ending

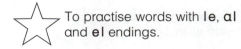

To practise words with le, al and el endings.

Remember: the ending that sounds like **apple** is usually spelt **le**. Ellie is a girl who only likes words that end in **le**. Circle all the **le** words:

Ellie likes pickles and apples, especially little ones. She drinks from a bottle and lives in a castle which is lit by candles in a circle. The handles all rattle because she has fiddled with them. Her room is a muddle but that doesn't trouble her.

Put the right el or al word in each space:

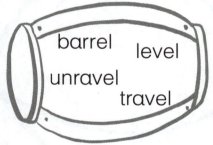

barrel level unravel travel

tropical metal pedal final

1. The _____ rolled away because the floor was not _____ .
2. We are going to _____ to the _____ rainforest.
3. The _____ stage of the race was to cross the _____ bridge.
4. When she began to_____, her scarf stuck in the wheel and started to _____ .

22

Spelling

To practise spelling words beginning with **de** or **di**.

Remember: you need to learn which words start with **de** and **di**.

Sort these words into the correct lists.

different   destroy   decided
difficulty   delicious
defend   disappoint   disembark
disappear
despair

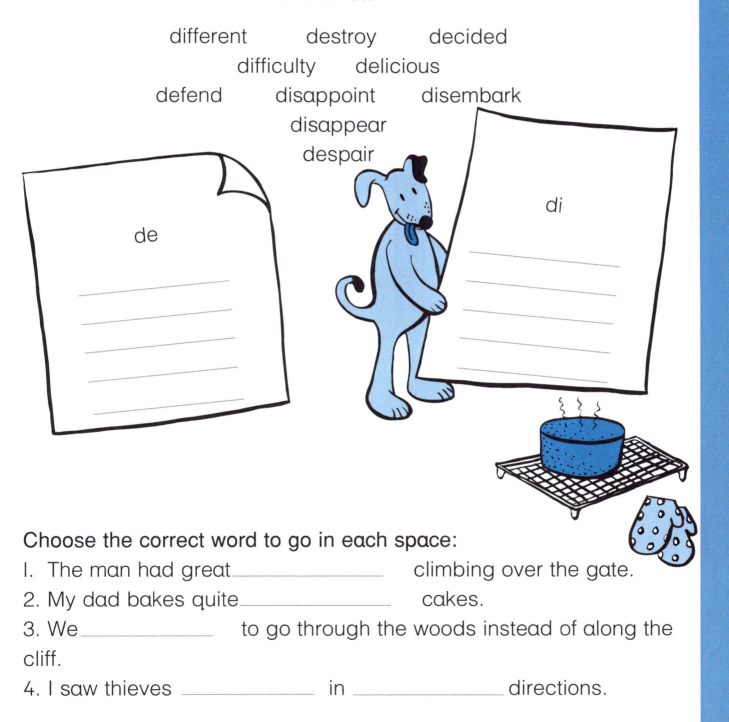

de

di

Choose the correct word to go in each space:

1. The man had great_____ climbing over the gate.
2. My dad bakes quite_____ cakes.
3. We_____ to go through the woods instead of along the cliff.
4. I saw thieves _____ in _____ directions.

The letter **w** – rules

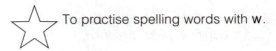

Remember: **w** is a letter which very often changes the sounds of **o** and **a**. For example: **want   ward   worm   won**

Can you finish this puzzle? The answers all contain **w**.

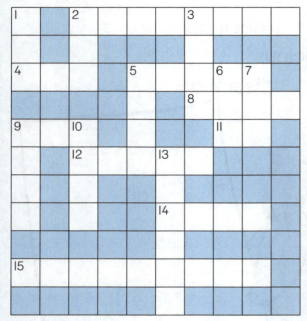

Across

2. Opposite of forward
4. Opposite of old
5. Opposite of better
8. When the sun rises
9. Past tense of 'is'
11. You and I
12. A clock you wear on your wrist
14. A fairy uses one to make spells
15. Thinking about

Down

1. Came first in the race
2. Do this when you finish performing
3. Made of letters
5. "_ _ _ _ do you want?"
6. Past tense of 'see'
7. A female sheep
9. Not cold
10. To exchange for something else
13. Someone who is not brave

Can you write one sentence using all these words?

worm   ward   warm   wandered

☆ To practise applying the 'i before e' rule.

Remember: 'i comes before e, except after c,' when the sound is 'eee'.
Can you learn to say it like a rhyme?

Fill the spaces with words that have **ie** or **ei**.
The sound is always 'eee'. Check you answers on page 3l.

A t _ _ _ _ _ _   has stolen my bike again.
Did you re_ _ _ _ _ _ _   a phone call from her?
I don't b _ _ _ _ _ _ _ _   in magic spells.
I tossed a pancake and a p_ _ _ _ _ _   went on the c _ _ _ _ _ _ _ _ .
My dad is a C_ _ _ _ _ _   Inspector in the police force.
Our visit was very br_ _ _ _ _ .

You need to remember these words which have **ei** instead of **ie**.

eight   w**ei**ght   h**ei**ght   r**ei**gn   n**ei**ghbour

w**ei**rd   s**ei**ze   for**ei**gn

Can you make a sentence that has all (or most) of those words in it?

_____

_____

_____

Apostrophes

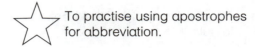

To practise using apostrophes for abbreviation.

Remember: we write an apostrophe where part of a word is missed out.

Match the words in the long carriage with the abbreviations in the short carriage.

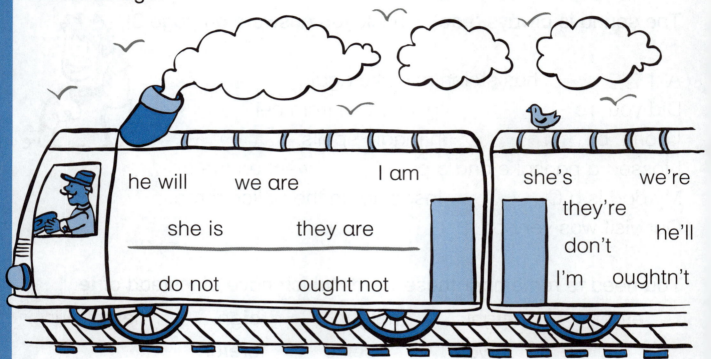

he will   we are   I am   she's   we're

she is   they are   they're
                                                        he'll
                                                don't
do not   ought not   I'm   oughtn't

Here's an odd one to learn: will not – won't

Write the shorter version of these words.
Always put the apostrophe where the letters are missing.

cannot _____   should not _____   it is _____

it has _____   you are _____   we will _____

we are _____   he is _____   they will _____

could not _____   is not _____   you will _____

 To practise using apostrophes for abbreviation.

Practising apostrophes

Write the shorter abbreviation in each space.

1. I _____ (did not) want to go to the zoo.

2. _____ (They are) trying to find a new house.

3. We _____ (will not) be back in time for tea.

4. You _____ (must not) watch television for too long.

5. I wonder where _____ (he is) going to stay.

6 I do wish he _____ (would not) do that.

Be careful about 'its'. It only has an apostrophe if it stands for 'it is' or 'it has'. Check this passage and put an apostrophe where it's needed.

The dog is wagging its tail because its waiting to go for a walk. Its raining at the moment so its got to wait a long time for its walk. The dog wishes its master didn't mind when its raining.

Homophones

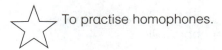

Homophones are words which sound the same.

where ("Where are you going?")   **wear** (to put on clothes)

night (the opposite of day)   **knight** (a fighter from long ago)

there ('Over there' or 'there are')   **their** (belonging to them)

they're (short for 'they are')

Put **there**, **their** or **they're** in the correct spaces.

We are going to stay at _____ house for two nights.

Are _____ any more sweets?

Why did you put it over _____ ?

I looked for your keys but I think _____ lost.

I think _____ house is beautiful.

Can you make up a sentence
which uses all of these words?
night   knight   wear   where

_____

_____

_____

_____

Fill each space with the correct word in brackets.

1.The_____(knight/night) wore rusty armour.

2.What shall I_____ (where/wear) tonight?

3._____(Where/Wear) did I put my gloves?

 To learn more homophones.

Here are some more. Do the same with these.

If you get any wrong, practise them. Draw a picture to show the meanings.

hair (on your head)   **hare** (animal like a rabbit)

pair (a set of two things)   **pear** (a fruit)

stair (a step, on the stairs) **stare** (to look without blinking)

fair (equally kind to both)   **fare** (what you pay on a bus or train)

1. I bought a _____ of ribbons for my_____.

2. It's rude to _____ .

3. The tortoise beat the _____ in a race.

4. She sat sadly on the top _____ .

5. There is one _____ left in the fruit bowl.

6. It's_____that some people should pay a cheaper_____.

hair	pair	stair	fair

hare	pear	stare	fare

Spelling

Proof-reading

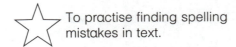

To practise finding spelling mistakes in text.

Rebecca has written this story. Can you help her find any mistakes before she gives it to her teacher? Circle the mistakes that you can find.

Tim disided to go a diferent way threw the woods. He knew should'nt but he had a wierd feeling that it would be intersting. Soon he came to stream. He sat down by the warter and took his shoes. In the burning sun, he allmost fell asleep. With dificulty, he stood up and rubbed his eyes.

Just then, Tim heard a terrifiing noise lick galloping hooves coming towords him. He rushed behind a tree to wotch. Along the path came what looked like a horse. The horse had one horn. This was a unicorn! Tim's freinds would'nt beleive in unicorns, so he decided not to tell anyone. He never did, but when he was a grown-up, he wrote it down and pretended it was just story.

There are 20 mistakes altogether but if you found 15 or more you did very well.

Page 31 will help you check any difficult words.

 To practise using a dictionary.

This dictionary page shows the spellings and plurals of lots of the words you've learnt in this book. How quickly can you find the word you want?

acrobat, acrobatics
almost
altogether
army, armies
beautiful
beginning
believe
boning, boned, bony
boy, boys
brief
bus, buses
careless
ceiling
celebrate
chief
child, children
coldness
comforting
creeping, creeper,
    creepy
day, days
decide, decided
dictionary, dictionaries
difficult, difficulty
disappear, disappeared
disappoint
donkey, donkeys
dutiful
echo, echoes
exciting
February

friends
funniness, funnily
galloping
half, halves
happening
helpfully
hero, heroes
holiday
hopeless, hopeful
hospital
house, houses
important
interesting
jumping, jumper,
    jumped, jumpy
life, lives
like, likely
loaf, loaves
love, loving, lover
    loved, loveliness
man, men
merciful
misunderstand
mystery
penniless
phoning, phoned
piece
pitiful
pretended
receive
remember

rush, rushes
scare, scaring, scared
    scary
sensible
silliness
smiling, smiler, smiled,
syllable, syllables
television
terrifying
thief
through
tickling, tickled, tickly
tomato, tomatoes
tomorrow
towards
typical
understand
unnecessary
usually
valley, valleys
watch
water
weird
whiteness
wife, wives
wolf, wolves
woman, women

Answers

page 2
whale: white, whiskers, wheel, whip, whether
cloud: loud, snout, proud, doubtful, couch

page 3
1. cabbage, 2. carrot, 3, caterpillar, 4. cauliflower, 5. clam, 6. crab, 7. crayfish
tomorrow, towards; disappear, disappoint; sensible, silliness; syllable, television; important, interesting; difficult, disappear

page 4
When Dad got to the shop, he forgot why he had come, so he went home to ask Mum. She just laughed. "You went to buy a notepad to help you remember things," she said.
blue: stone, easy, bike
red: umbrella, hut, bag, doll

page 5
rate, site, note, hate, pine, spine, tube, tripe
1. cone, 2. sale, 3. tune, 4. diver, 5. skate, 6. prize
Shaded letters: clever

page 6
e.g. The rich witch had an itch, which was very painful.
such, watch, match, catch, pitch, coach, bench, each, much, which

page 7
fridge, hedgehog, cage, age, lodge, stodge, page, stage, gorge, edge, huge, dodge, porridge, wedge, rage, wage

page 8
3, 3, 3, 3
1. tomorrow, 2. understand, 3. important, 4. disappeared, 5. holiday, 6. remember, 7. hospital

page 9
po/ta/to; cal/cu/la/tor; am/bu/lance
beginning, celebrate, exciting, acrobat, disappoint, typical, comforting, mystery

page 10
phoning, phoned; jumping, jumper, jumped, jumpy; smiling, smiler, smiled; boning, boned, bony; creeping, creeper, creepy; tickling, tickled, tickly; scaring, scared, scary; loving, lover, loved

page 11
funnily, silliness, pitiful, loveliness
hopeless, careless, penniless; merciful, dutiful, beautiful; likely, usually, helpfully; funniness, coldness, whiteness

page 12
Although you were helpful it was also useful to ask my dad.
1. also, 2. useful, 3. until, 4. hopeful, 5. almost, 6. cupful, 7. altogether, 8. handful
Word in blue column: although

page 13
prove, act, grace, prompt, fair, load, guide, lift, ease
unnecessary/unaware; misbehave/mislead; impossible/impatient; underground/undertaker; telephone/telescope; disagree/dishonest
(Your child may think of other words, these are only suggestions)

page 16
'ur' : turn, burnt, hurt, turned
'ir' : bird, circus, third, thirty
'ear' : learnt, earn, searching, heard

page 17
enormous - huge; courageous - brave; cautious - very careful; jealous - wanting what someone else has got; precious - worth a lot of money; luxurious - rich, comfortable and expensive; dangerous - not safe, risky; curious - strange, can also mean 'nosey'; anxious - worried; famous - well-known by lots of people

page 18
monkeys, bushes, tomatoes
dictionaries, words, boys

page 20
sight, sighting, bright, brighter, fight, fighting, fighter, fright, tight, tighter, light, lighter, night, thigh (Your child may find more words)
thought, enough, dough, although, ought, bought

page 21
thistle, wheel, bomb, autumn, listen, ghost, column, lamb, hymn, thumb, bristle, which
b: bomb, lamb, thumb
t: thistle, listen, bristle
h: wheel, ghost, which
n: autumn, column, hymn

page 22
le words: pickles, apples, little, bottle, castle, candles, circle, handles, rattle, fiddled, muddle, trouble
1. barrel, level, 2. travel, tropical, 3. final, metal, 4. pedal, unravel

page 23
de: destroy, decided, delicious, defend, despair
di: different, difficulty, disappoint, disembark, disappear
1. difficulty, 2, delicious, 3. decided, 4. disappear, different

page 24
Across: 2. backward, 4. new, 5. worse, 8. dawn, 9. was, 11. we, 12. watch, 14. wand, 15. wondering
Down: 1. won, 2. bow, 3. word, 5. what, 6. saw, 7. ewe, 9. warm, 10. swap, 13. coward

page 25
thief, receive, believe, piece, ceiling, Chief, brief

page 26
he will - he'll; we are - we're; I am - I'm; she is - she's; they are - they're; do not - don't; ought not - oughtn't
cannot - can't; should not - shouldn't; it is - it's; it has - it's; you are - you're; we will - we'll; we are - we're; he is - he's; they will - they'll; could not - couldn't; is not - isn't; you will - you'll

page 27
1. didn't, 2. They're, 3. won't, 4. mustn't, 5. he's, 6. wouldn't
The dog is wagging its tail because it's waiting to go for a walk. It's raining at the moment so it's got to wait a long time for its walk. The dog wishes its master didn't mind when it's raining.

page 28
their, there, there, they're, their
1. knight, 2. wear, 3. Where

page 29
1. pair, hair, 2. stare, 3. hare, 4. stair, 5. pear, 6. fair, fare

page 30
Tim decided to go a different way through the woods. He knew he shouldn't but he had a weird feeling that it would be interesting. Soon he came to a stream. He sat down by the water and took his shoes off. In the burning sun, he almost fell asleep. With difficulty, he stood up and rubbed his eyes.
Just then, Tim heard a terrifying noise like galloping hooves coming towards him. He rushed behind a tree to watch. Along the path came what looked like a horse. The horse had one horn. This was a unicorn! Tim's friends wouldn't believe in unicorns, so he decided not to tell anyone. He never did, but when he was a grown-up, he wrote it down and pretended it was just a story.